Man and Materials Series

Man and Materials: COAL
Man and Materials: GAS
Man and Materials: MINERALS
Man and Materials: OIL
Man and Materials: PLASTICS
Man and Materials: STONE

An Addisonian Press Book

© 1975 Macmillan Education Limited of London
Designed by Robert Updegraff
Printed in Spain
First Printing

Photographic Acknowledgements
Airfix Products; Bakelite Xylonite; British Celanese; British
Industrial Plastics; BP Educational Service; Du Pont Co. (UK);
General Electric Research and Development Center, U.S.A.;
Hoechst Chemicals; National Plastics; Shell;
Tower Housewares; Robert Updegraff.

Library of Congress Cataloging in Publication Data
Ridpath, Ian.
    Man and materials: plastics.
    SUMMARY: Discusses the history, composition, pro-
duction, uses, advantages, and disadvantages of plastics
and the distinctive properties of various kinds.
    1. Plastics—Juvenile literature. [1. Plastics]
I. Title.
TP1125.R5   1975   668'.4   74-10567
ISBN 0-201-09034-1

Man and Materials

PLASTICS

compiled under the general editorship of Ian Ridpath

▲▲ Addison-Wesley

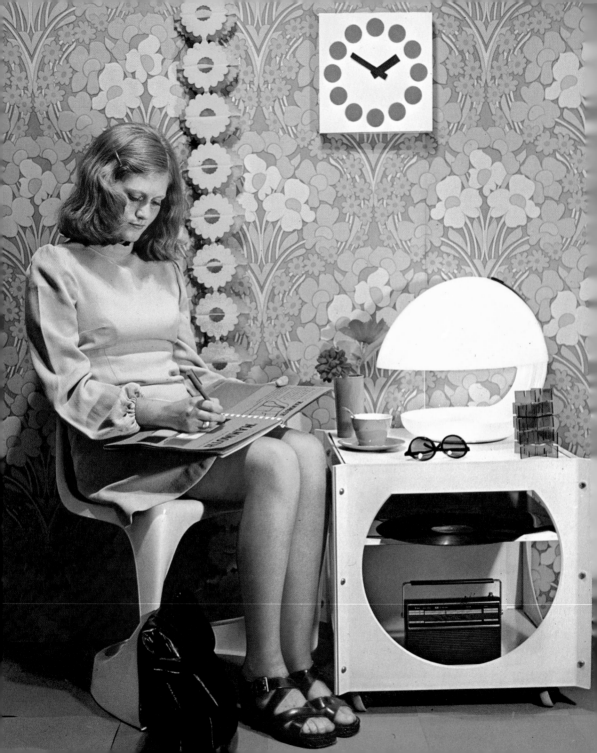

What are Plastics?

We see plastics all around us—in the home, at school, and at work. There is no single material called 'plastic'. Chemists and engineers have created a whole series of plastics, each with a slightly different composition. These often have different uses, but most plastics have several similarities.

Plastics do not rot or corrode, like wood and metal. Most are good insulants: they block the passage of electricity and heat. Plastics are light in weight, and they can be made in many different colors.

Plastics are easy to mold. The word 'plastic' means soft. When the material is heated, it becomes soft and can be molded. Complicated shapes can be easily formed from plastics.

At left: Plastics are often colorful and usually have a shiny finish. They can be soft and pliable or hard and shockproof. They have many uses, some of which are shown in the picture. Everything (except the girl) is made out of plastics: the artificial fibres of her clothing, the wallpaper's surface, floor tiles, furniture, handbag and shoes, the clock, LP records, transistor radio case, pen, cup and saucer, sunglasses, and flowers.

What Plastics are Made of

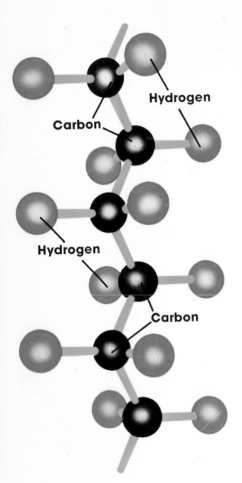

Plastics are based on carbon atoms. In plastics, the carbon atoms are usually joined to hydrogen, often with other atoms such as oxygen and nitrogen. Such atoms are very common on Earth. It is the way in which they are joined that is important.

Atoms join into groups called *molecules*. Each chemical has a different kind of molecule. The properties of plastics depend on the molecules of which they are composed, and the way in which these are linked.

The molecules in plastics are linked into long chains called *polymers*, meaning 'lots of parts'. A typical polymer chain can contain tens of thousands of molecules. These chains arise because carbon easily joins with other atoms.

Above: A diagram of a polymer called ethylene. It is made by linking identical molecules of carbon and hydrogen.

4

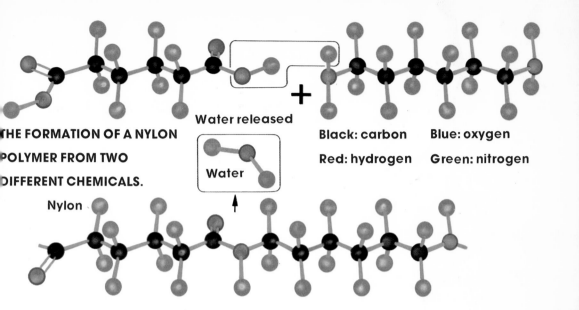

THE FORMATION OF A NYLON POLYMER FROM TWO DIFFERENT CHEMICALS.

Water released

Water

Nylon

Black: carbon   Blue: oxygen

Red: hydrogen   Green: nitrogen

When the molecules are turned into polymers (polymerized), they form a thick liquid or, more usually, a solid material. This can take the form of a powder, or it may be chopped up into pellets or beads. The material is then known as *raw plastics*—it has not yet been shaped into the finished article.

The composition of many plastics is evident from their names. Many plastics start with 'poly' followed by the name of the molecule that has been polymerized —for example 'polyethylene'.

Below: A handful of raw plastic pellets.

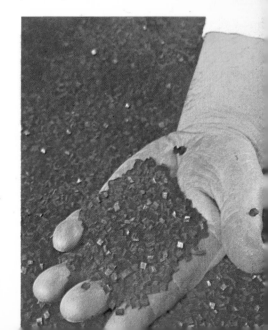

Improving on Nature

The vast majority of the substances we call plastics are man-made. But a few plastics-like materials occur naturally. An example is amber, the solidified resin from trees.

Natural plastics are little used today. But some man-made plastics are modifications of natural polymers. One such material is cellulose. This is composed of long chains of carbon, hydrogen, and oxygen molecules and is found in all plants and vegetables.

Above: One natural plastic is amber, a solidified resin from trees. Insects often become stuck in the amber and you can sometimes find them embedded in it. Right: Cellulose sheets can be made by cutting a solid cellulose block (celluloid) with a sharp knife.

The major source of cellulose was originally cotton, but most cellulose today is processed from wood. It can be made into solid celluloid, or thin transparent cellophane sheeting used for packaging.

Rubber is an important polymer. It is strengthened by *vulcanizing*—heating it with sulphur. Adding more sulphur turns it into semi-solid ebonite. Scientists can now make many kinds of synthetic (man-made) rubber.

Above: A remarkable development, based on the natural ability of fish to breathe through gills. Silicone rubber, a synthetic polymer, is completely waterproof but it allows air through. The rabbit breathes air that passes from the surrounding water through the rubber membrane.

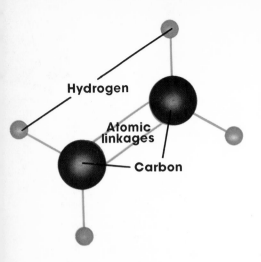

Hydrogen

Atomic linkages

Carbon

The construction of an ethylene molecule (above) and a propylene molecule (below).

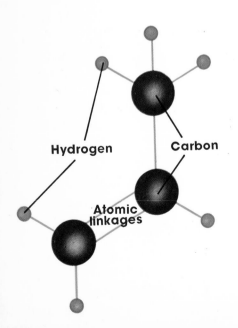

Hydrogen

Carbon

Atomic linkages

Making Plastics

To make plastics, chemists assembl molecules like building blocks. Thei main materials are *hydrocarbons* fron oil, gas, or coal. These are molecule composed of different numbers of carbor and hydrogen atoms.

One of the most useful hydrocarbon is the gas *ethylene*. Its formula is writter C_2H_4. It is composed of two atoms o carbon (symbol C) and four atoms o hydrogen (symbol H).

Ethylene is obtained from the ligh oil called naphtha. It is separated b heating the naphtha, so that the hydro carbons break up into smaller molecules This process is called *cracking*.

Other hydrocarbons, with differin numbers of hydrogen and carbon atoms are produced by cracking naphtha. Thes include methane, propylene, and buta diene.

What happens next largely depends on the polymer chemist's ingenuity. He can add and subtract hydrogen and carbon atoms, and introduce other sorts of atoms. This gives him a nearly-limitless range of molecules to polymerize.

Not all of these plastics will be of use, but many of them form valuable new materials. Research continues, since it is probable that some of the most useful polymers have not yet been discovered.

Top left: Teflon, a highly resistant plastic, is used as the non-stick coating on kitchenware.
Above left: Plastic film is used to wrap foods.
Above: Sheets of Mylar plastic, less than one-tenth of a millimeter thick, being used to carry a very heavy load.

Thermoplastics

There are two types of plastics. They differ in the way that their molecule chains behave when heated. The most common type is called *thermoplastics*.

Thermoplastics can be softened or melted by heating, but their molecule chains are not altered chemically. When the thermoplastic material cools, the molecule chains remain unconnected to their neighboring chains.

Thermoplastics can be melted down and recast into fresh shapes. Many thermoplastics have quite low melting points. They cannot be used in situations where they would become hot and soft.

Above left: A cover for plants, made from polypropylene.
Above: Polyethylene crates for bottles.
Below: Contact lenses are made from Perspex.

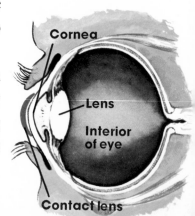

Cornea

Lens

Interior of eye

Contact lens

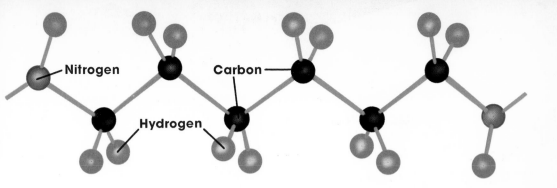

Nitrogen

Carbon

Hydrogen

Above: The structure of a Nylon molecule.

Below: A spiral chute of polypropylene sheet.

Polystyrene was the first thermoplastic to be produced, in 1929. Soon afterwards PVC and polyethylene were developed. These are still three of the most common thermoplastics.

In 1938, the American chemical firm of Du Pont began to produce the world's first artificial fibre—Nylon. This is the most common synthetic fibre, and is also widely used in its solid form.

Acrylic plastics are derived from acrylic acid. They include the transparent sheet known as Perspex or Plexiglas. Other acrylic plastics are synthetic fibres which are sold under trade names such as Acrilan and Orlon.

Polypropylene is an increasingly popular thermoplastic. It is similar to polyethylene, but is stronger and withstands higher temperatures.

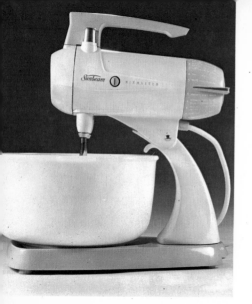

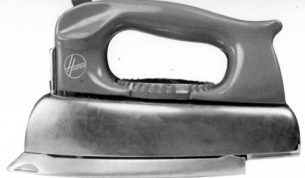

Thermosetting Plastics

These pictures show some of the many uses of thermosetting plastics. They can be made more attractive by chemical coloring.

Polymers that make up the second type of plastics are called *thermosetting plastics*. When they are heated they undergo a chemical change. Their molecule chains form chemical cross-linkages when hot, making them three-dimensional polymers. When they cool, thermosetting plastics become hard and rigid. They cannot be softened again.

Thermosetting plastics can withstand very high temperatures. They are often used to make saucepan handles and ashtrays. The cross-linkages between their molecule chains make thermosetting plastics strong and chemically stable.

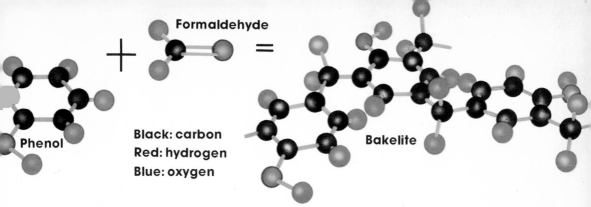

Formaldehyde

Phenol

Black: carbon
Red: hydrogen
Blue: oxygen

Bakelite

The first fully man-made plastic was a thermosetting material called Bakelite. This was developed in 1907 by the Belgian-born chemist Leo Baekeland. Because of its excellent insulation properties, it is a very useful material for insulating electrical goods.

Bakelite is one of the so-called *phenolic* plastics. It is made from chemicals that include phenol (carbolic acid).

Natural Bakelite has a dark color. The largest group of thermosetting polymers, called *amino* plastics, often have chemicals added to them to make them brightly colored. They are used to make telephone cases, and cups and saucers.

Some thermosetting materials, called epoxy resins and polyesters, harden naturally without heat. They are used as adhesives, among other things.

Above: The formation of Bakelite from two different chemicals.

Below: Leo Baekeland.

Polyethylene

Polyethylene is one of the world's most widely used plastics. As the name indicates, it is made up of many molecules of ethylene. Polyethylene is a thermoplastic material with a smooth, waxy texture. Its name is often shortened to *polythene*.

Polyethylene was discovered in 1933. It is tough, waterproof, and a good electrical insulant—properties which make it suitable for a wide variety of uses. Most plastic bags and sheets are made out of polyethylene.

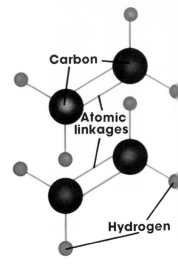

Molecules of ethylene (above) can join into polymer chains (above right) when their carbon linkages alter.

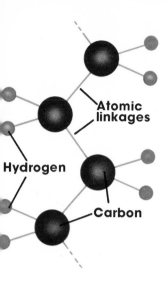

Atomic linkages

Hydrogen

Carbon

elow: Many familiar
objects in the home are
made of polyethylene
(polythene), a smooth,
waxy plastic.

In 1953, a slightly different type of polyethylene was discovered. This is called high-density polyethylene.

The two forms of polyethylene have the same composition, but in the high-density type the polymer chains are closer together. This type has greater resistance to heat and greater strength. It is used in the home for cups, bowls, buckets, and wastebaskets.

The low-density type is made by compressing ethylene molecules at pressures 1000 or 2000 times that of the Earth's atmosphere. The high-density type is made at much lower pressures using chemicals to help the reaction.

PVC

Polyvinylchloride is the full name of one of our most useful insulants and water-proofers. This long name is usually shortened to PVC, or sometimes it is called *vinyl*.

PVC is a thermoplastic. It is made from a combination of the gases ethylene and chlorine. When these gases react, they form a substance which is called ethylene dichloride.

The ethylene dichloride is strongly heated to split up the molecules into vinyl chloride gas. The vinyl chloride molecules are then joined together to make the PVC polymer.

Some of the many items which are made from PVC or in which PVC plays a part. PVC polymer is made under pressure from vinyl chloride molecules.

Vinyl chloride is put under pressure to turn it into a polymer. A chemical stabilizer is added to the polymer so that the PVC can be molded. Otherwise it would change form when heated. The PVC can then be molded into rigid, colorless articles. To make flexible items a substance called a plasticizer is added to the polymer. Color may be added later.

Molding machines turn the PVC into various shapes. Common uses are in gutters and pipes, and the insulation of electrical cables. PVC sheets are turned into plastic mackintoshes.

Thin layers of PVC are used to make washable 'vinyl' wallpapers. Thicker layers make soles for shoes and vinyl tiles.

Polystyrene

Polystyrene is mostly used for packaging and particularly for food storage. It comes in three types. Toughened polystyrene contains some rubber, and is used for cups in vending machines. Transparent polystyrene is used for the barrels of ball-point pens. Expanded polystyrene is used as ceiling tiles.

Polystyrene is a polymer of styrene. This material can be produced by combining ethylene gas with benzene, a light oil from petroleum.

Styrene can be polymerized in two ways. In the first method, liquid polystyrene can be produced in a heated tower. Pigments and the rubber filler are added where necessary. It is squeezed out in long strands like spaghetti, which are then chopped into small pellets. The second way is to stir the styrene into hot water to polymerize it into solid beads.

Examples of the use of Polystyrene as packaging material. The items are on ceiling tiles made of expanded polystyrene.

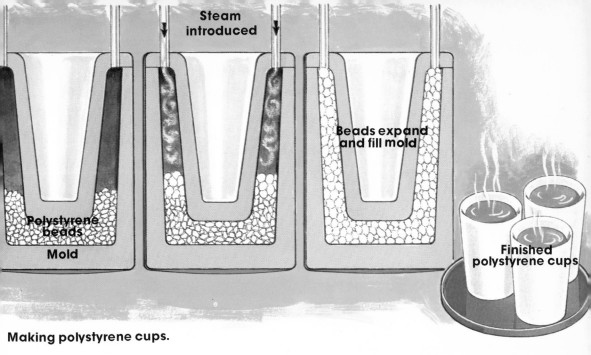

Steam introduced

Beads expand
and fill mold

Polystyrene beads

Mold

Finished
polystyrene cups

Making polystyrene cups.

Below: Polystyrene beads.

Expanded polystyrene is made by injecting a *foaming agent* (a substance that releases gas) into the polymer. When heated, the gas causes the pellets to expand like tiny balloons. These stick together in a mold to form a finished object.

Toughened polystyrene is often used as tubs to hold food. Many of the fittings in the interior of refrigerators are made of polystyrene. Polystyrene is affected by heat and discolors in strong daylight.

Injection Molding

When the raw polymer has been produced, it must be shaped to form the required object. There are several ways of doing this. The method chosen depends on the shape of the article required and the type of plastic which is used.

Some of the most familiar shapes are made by the technique called *injection molding*. It is similar to the casting of metal in a mold. Injection molding is so named because a machine injects the plastic into a mold.

Injection molding can produce accurate shapes, such as watch gears (above), kit parts (below) and calculator machine parts (below left).

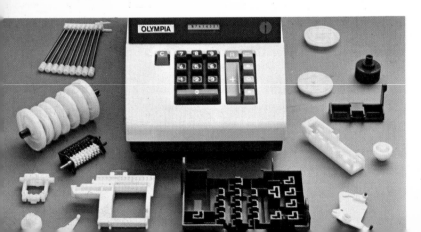

INJECTION MOLDING MACHINE

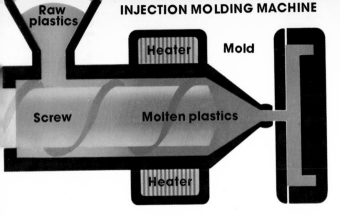

Raw plastics

Heater

Mold

Screw

Molten plastics

Heater

The raw material is fed into a hopper. It falls into a cylinder containing a spiral feeder, which turns to force the polymer into the mold. Heaters around the cylinder are used to melt the material into a liquid.

After injection, the polymer hardens into the shape of the mold. The mold is then opened and the finished object is taken out. An object shaped by injection molding usually has a raised ring where the molten plastics were forced into the joint of the mold.

Injection molding is used for thermoplastic materials. Familiar examples are wastebaskets, bowls, buckets, cups, and food cartons. Very accurate shapes, including plastic gears and machine parts, can be produced by injection molding.

Above: Pouring raw plastics into an injection mold.
Below: Removing finished injection moldings.

Extrusion Molding

In an extrusion molding machine, molten plastics are squeezed through an opening like toothpaste out a tube. The shape of the opening determines the shape of the finished plastic article.

Another familiar method of making objects from plastics is called *extrusion*. In this method, the molten polymer is extruded through an opening, called a die. As in injection molding, a screw or plunger forces raw polymer towards the molding head. Heaters turn the material into a liquid.

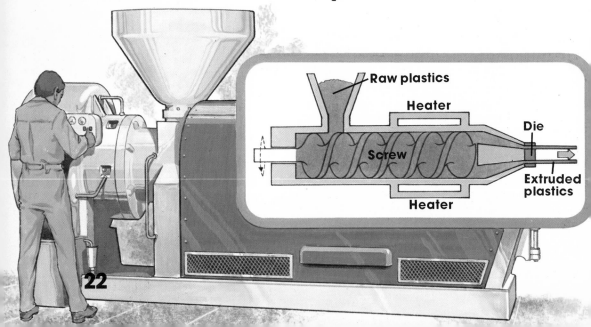

Raw plastics

Heater

Screw

Die

Extruded plastics

Heater

The molten material is extruded into the required shape as it passes through the die. Once it has passed through, the polymer runs along a supporting belt or trough where it is cooled and hardened by blasts of air or water.

The extrusion method is used for shaping PVC and other thermoplastics.

A wide variety of shapes can be produced in this way. They usually come out in continuous lengths, which are then cut up as required. A familiar example is plastic sheeting, which can also be made by flattening the molten polymer between rollers.

PVC sheets, pipes, and guttering are produced by extrusion. Wires and cables passing through an extrusion machine are coated with layers of PVC or polyethylene insulation.

Extrusion is also the method that is used to turn thermoplastics into fine fibres. These are often woven into clothing and furnishing fabrics.

Above: The head of an extrusion machine producing plastic strip. Below: Some products made by extrusion.

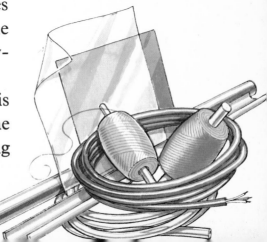

Blow-molding

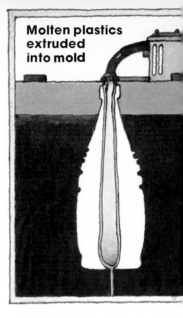

Molten plastics extruded into mold

Plastics are important for making containers. Bottles, boxes, tubes, sachets, and many other containers are made by a technique called *blow-molding*. A familiar example is the fruit-juice bottle, now commonly made from PVC.

The PVC can be blown into a bottle-shape in a similar way to a balloon being inflated. First, a thin cylinder of plastics, or sometimes two thin sheets, is extruded from a die. A mold is closed round one end to seal it.

Then a sudden blast of air or steam blows out the material into the shape of the mold. Water circulates through the mold walls to cool the material and help it to set quickly.

Above: Stages in blow molding. Air is blown into a thin cylinder of plastics that has been extruded into the mold.

Right: Children's toothpaste tubes made by blow molding.

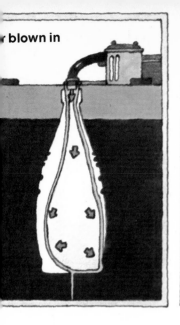
blown in

Plastic takes up shape of mold

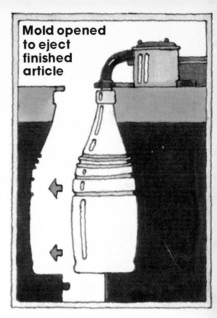
Mold opened to eject finished article

Many hollow objects, including dolls, are made by blow-molding plastics.

Other kinds of packaging material are made out of foamed plastics. These include expanded polystyrene (see page 19). They are often used as substitutes for cork and balsawood. Expanded polystyrene is particularly useful as a packaging material because it is light in weight and bulky and crushproof.

The air spaces in expanded plastics make them excellent heat and sound insulants. Polyurethane foams, commonly known as 'foam rubber', are often used as filling material for cushions.

Below: Expanded plastic foam, often called foam rubber, makes an excellent insulant. It is also used as a filling material for cushions and packaging.

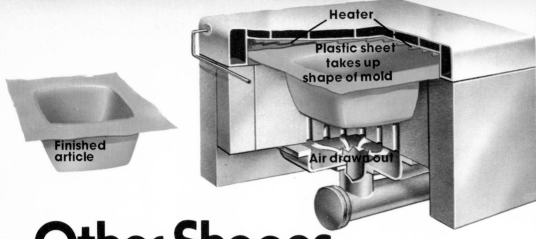

Heater

Plastic sheet takes up shape of mold

Air drawn out

Finished article

Other Shapes

Thermoplastics may also be shaped by a technique known as *vacuum forming*. A sheet of plastics is first produced, and laid over a hollow mold.

The sheet is heated to soften the material. Air is then sucked out of the mold to produce a partial vacuum. The sheet is drawn into the mold by suction, and in this way it takes up the shape of the mold. Objects such as trays are produced by this technique.

Another method that is used for shaping the thermosetting types of plastics is called *compression molding*. Molten polymer is heated in a mold, and squashed into shape by another mold which presses down on it.

Above: A molten plastic sheet can be shaped by vacuum forming.

Below: Saucepan handles are made from thermosetting plastics by compression molding.

26

Right: Hollow objects are often made from thermoplastics by rotational casting. Raw plastics are put into a mold which is rotated rapidly in an oven.

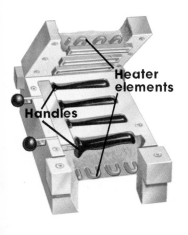

Above: In a compression molding machine, the two halves of the mold are pressed together to shape the polymer into saucepan handles.

The complex chains of thermosetting plastics are formed while the molten material is in the mold. It hardens directly into the required shape. This method is used for molding various kinds of electrical fittings.

Hollow objects, such as beachballs, are made from thermoplastics. Raw plastics powder is fed into a spherical mold which is then put in an oven. The mold is rotated rapidly inside the oven, so that the polymer takes up the shape of the inside of the mold. The heat of the oven melts the polymer, and when it cools it retains its shape. This is known as *rotational casting.*

27

Sheet and Coating Plastics

Molten plastics can be rolled into sheets in a large machine like a mangle. This is called *calendering*. The raw polymer is melted by passing between heated rollers, and forms a thick sheet. This is squeezed to the required thickness and decorated by other rollers. Then it is cooled.

Plastics are coated onto backing material, such as fabric or paper, by calendering. As the material passes between the rollers, molten polymer is spread on.

Above: A calendering machine is used to produce plastic sheets. Below: The hot and cold rollers for calendering.

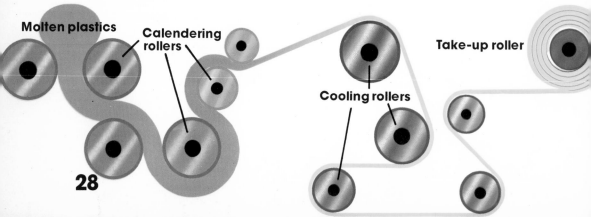

Molten plastics

Calendering rollers

Take-up roller

Cooling rollers

Another way of coating objects is *dip molding*. Rubber gloves and boots are made by dipping the fabric liner into a molten mass of polymer.

Reinforced sheets of plastics, called *laminates*, are made from layers of thermo-setting plastics with cloth or paper. The layers are bonded together in a hot press. Laminates are often used for kitchen table tops.

For complex shapes, plastics can be produced on a mold by hand. Glass-fibre moldings, first of all mixed with thermosetting adhesives, are made in this way. Boat hulls, car bodies, and other materials previously made of metal are now made of fibre-reinforced plastics.

Above: A thermosetting plastic, known as a resin, being poured onto glass fibres. When the resin hardens, it will bond the fibres together strongly.

Right: After calendering, plastic sheet can have a pattern printed on it by other rollers. Vinyl wallpapers can be coated in this way.

Plain sheet **Printing rollers** **Printed sheet wound up into roll**

Where Plastics are Made

Amount of plastics produced in thousands of metric tons per month.

Australia	37
Austria	21
Canada	67
Czechoslovakia	32
France	175
East Germany	38
West Germany	542
India	9
Italy	201
Japan	464
Netherlands	155
Poland	36
Romania	21
Spain	54
USSR	187
UK	143
USA	806

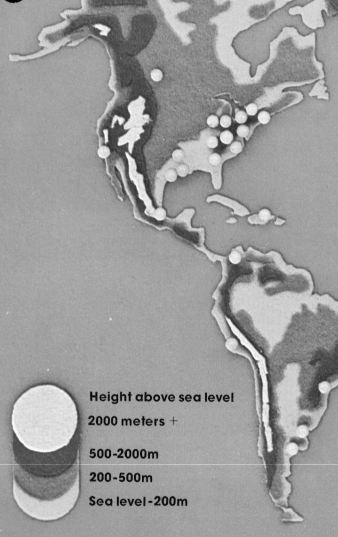

Height above sea level

2000 meters +

500-2000m

200-500m

Sea level-200m

30

MAJOR PRODUCTION CENTERS

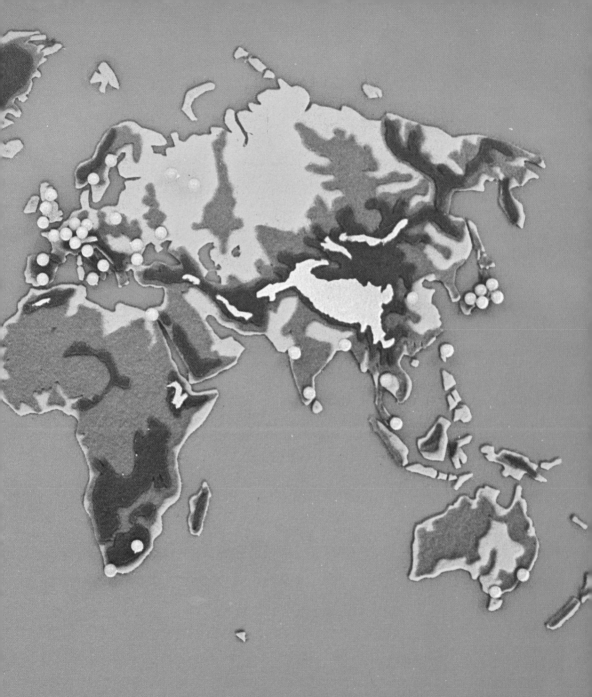

Plastics and the Environment

One of the advantages of plastics is that they do not corrode or rot. But this makes them a major pollution problem, for waste plastics do not decay. About 5000 million kilograms of waste plastics are thrown away every year in the U.S.A. and the amount is increasing.

One solution is plastics that are only temporarily stable and decay after a few years. The simplest solution, however, is to encourage people to return the waste plastics for melting down and recycling.

Plastics provide a major waste-disposal problem. In 30 years time, the output of plastics may be greater than that of steel. All the objects shown at the start of the book now look a mess on a rubbish heap. Unlike most other material they will not decay natura

Index